Wakefield Press

A Fingerpost for Rembrandt

Peter Lloyd was born in the English Midlands and emigrated to Australia in the late 1970s. Most of his working life has been dedicated to providing housing for the under-privileged. He lives in the Adelaide Hills and is married with two children. Peter has had work published in Australia, Canada, the United States, the United Kingdom and France.

T0363970

a fingerpost for Rembrandt

Peter Lloyd

**Wakefield
Press**

Wakefield Press
1 The Parade West
Kent Town
South Australia 5067
www.wakefieldpress.com.au

First published 2004
Copyright © Peter Lloyd, 2004

Typeset by Ryan Paine, Wakefield Press
Printed and bound by Hyde Park Press

National Library of Australia
Cataloguing-in-publication entry

Lloyd, Peter, 1930– .
A fingerpost for Rembrandt.

ISBN 1 86254 652 5.

I. Title.

A821.3

Publication of this book was assisted by the
Commonwealth Government through the
Australia Council, its arts funding and advisory body.

To my dearest wife, Rosa — rest in peace

2 October 2004

Contents

Crimewatch

From bulldozed moonscapes /
low-grade estates on the hill,

— two cops observe essential lifeblood
flowing into grids East-West

— heavy arterial violence of the Freeway
thundering past.

Two cops on Crimewatch.

Dark glasses, guns.

This is what they do best.

This is their job.

The big transports.
The armoured cars.

Overhead, electrical impulses
criss-cross the curvature of the world

like searchlights in the dark,

wham! bombarding the city, glass skyscrapers,
direct hits! Blue-violet rays —

sweet glowing waves of hot money.

Outlaw Country

. . . and after The Cutting, comes heavy-shit / Graffiti-Junction,

Voodoo-doo-doo land —

over the demolitions you'd never walk alone,
Dock St., Newcastle Rd., Mile End:

the railway slices through
haze of Scrapyards, Cranes, Concrete Works:

Spraycan-opolis —

where long Intercities roll-past, points grinding, mile after mile of
rainbow opus of howling and nickelodeon galactics,

heavy-metal-phantom warriors stare from walls /
abandoned rolling stock.

By day, first class — the living rich
with ghosts of the living-dead glide past —

Beaudelaire's Flowers of Evil, Rimbaud's sonic envelope,*
Songs of Verlaine and Hell;

light — pure glints from smashed sinks, sewage pipes,
purple / green chemical lakes . . .

By night, cop car territory —

deep sky over frozen rails,
jagged tips

and wild dogs giving birth —

pure magic.

*Inspiration through disorientation of the senses

The Poster

Sunset — and in Blake's ever-starfix on the heavens —

> *'. . . the Cloud that opens, rolling apart before the Throne &
>   before the New Heaven & the New Earth . . .'*

bells ring for Evensong:

15 cwt. Tenor bang! rolls, bang!
bells C sharp B > A > G sharp F sharp

as a Cathedral spasms into showtime-zoom-flights over the city,
sudden explosion of pigeon wings . . .

Puritans, English hymn books, tombs, saints' bones, locutary, cloisters.
It's all in the Gothic light. A soaring, upward force, scattering

of stained glass windows over Woolworth's, clouds, the By-pass,
dirty washing from the launderette flapping on the Reredos —

a dazzle / blue / crimson / yellow puddles in spire-shadows, sun's last
'. . . folding like Scrolls of the Enormous Volume of Heaven & Earth . . .'

— stunned by light, amazed — as we dodge a kid from the Uni. cycling past,

JESUS CUNT

spraycanned back of his jacket.

A ripped poster in the bus shelter flaps

    w
        uf   C
           Usmal.

G
     Tiger.

           Dillon.

www dot war against torture dot info.

The new Latin.

Inside Blues

Well, she's got the horrors,
no-escape-old-lady's got the inside blues —

old lady in Alzheimer Ho-tel — she's got the blue-green horrors,
spermy spiders in her hair,

hanging from the ceiling in a cave of red ribbons,
mumbling and screaming like a bat,

old lady's hanging like a bat in a cave of ribbons in the dark:

how many times
how many times

in the fiery wingfall beat of stars,

in midnight Alzheimer Ho-tel where broken folk are listening to the dark?

Fasten your hairband, Alice,

there are footsteps on the stairs,
many footsteps on the stairs —

but hark!
                who journeys long and well

O yes!

      that's music not screaming

      where black dogs howl top of the stairs,
      where yellowdog ghosts howl at poor blind souls flapping around
          their feet . . .

backwards and forwards she swings,
crooning and singing in the dark,

backwards and forwards beating her leather wings.

Someday her prince may come.

Migrants Dreaming

— Would migrants dreaming —
  would the Gitanjali Song Offering

know what to do with these exiled moments

of peacock bride-silks, waterfalls lustred with vanilla?
Purple-in-the-mist drifts over rooftops: windows melt into an Indian
  poem . . .

as 'a lotus song in the jewel, her naked breasts play counterpoint to flutes'
and the sound of zithers drifting up the street;

— fragile — delicate as a sari of distance and silences,

Kashmir dreams itself over again . . . a fading light — but outside time,
  another life
'meeting the same souls and bodies that distantly were yours . . .'

— until a bell rings through a falling dark of window boxes
and naked children fall into an ossuary of golden twigs and fragile
  wishbones for the dead.

The surreal vanishes.

A door bangs back into reality.
And cold rain suddenly spatters through broken glass.

From a bulldozed squat in time —

hunched shadows from a window watch like cripples from the wall . . .

Flutterings

Soot-red / greys / evening of snake-head orange lights.

Mist-distortions,
cankered mouths drained out

round the true God's palace anathema to filthy impersonators:

traffic swirls: black-stone,
caffs for the homeless

where fungal-rot takes what is now cold breath and unburied
poison of neglect in shadow of the spire. Dark aisles below,

(in strict rubric crimson of the well-beloved and cripples)

above the altar, timeless
and past all future — gold zeniths of the sacred cloth

break into vague futurities / disputations / dissolutions,
masked saints among the Carousel and the Life to Be

with hyphae of lead-gray in a house of spores and settling cavities.

They blow past from the misty street — unhappy spirits,
darkness hanging over the city in a dried bag of nerves,

but toughing out the rage, Ishmaels of the lost, heads bent,
searching the gutters, among fag-ends and crushed tins

for the key somewhere to the Universe . . .

* * *

. . . they drift by, old sacks, plastic bags, feet sticking out

from the dark — all night-sounds in the Churchyard,

vague, small-flutterings, restless, never-settling
but vanishing, reappearing again, here-there,

among lopsided graves, broken pillars, outlines of bitter purple
fading into shadow-brown —

and are they souls or birds?

Bread

The half-life of Uranium / the price of gold —

static crackles — screams of *Schnell! Schnell!*
urgent as Stockhausen's fracture-ese, dissonances

spinning through foodchains,
and ancient rat-holes in a crumbling sky.

Thus — Fukuyama's *'. . . end of history —*
. . . in Liberal Democracy, the planet has reached its supreme destiny . . .'

Old segues and post modernism in transit,
a screech of tin violins hurled through broken headlights,

dissolutions, beggars, deaths and topsoil blowing.

By iron railings, churchyards
at street ends — no moon! Over wastelands,

the terrible weird glow of drums —
Shiva's death-grip at the end of things . . .

— Tunes played on bootleg tapes
at rusting traffic lights, Fanfare to the Common Man — with

Giant Trumpets of Destiny pouring massive red / green energy
from one Universe to another,

dart-dancing through the mist —

   (cogs of hyper-world going round)

with incidental,
clatter
of
bottles,

back of the Hoo Fong chippy —

Dwarfwoman

hobbling away
through a skein of blackheads

with a fistful of bread.

The Hut

Come Doomsday — when flash fires envelop encyclopedic prophecies and
   a thunder-heaped rubbish dump
                        wreathes smoke and exploding oil drums,

at world-top: the Keeper's tin shack
under attack

from earth-movers obscured by planetary dust:
and purple sun eclipse . . .

huge gulls, festooned with sea-harps, circle,
pecking viciously at the window

where the old Keeper, on a stool propped with bricks,
picks out a tune on his harmonium from a half-burnt sheet of music —

Procedentem sponsum
de thalamo
   Laude digne prolem . . .

To the bridegroom proceeding
from the bridal chamber —
   with fitting praise . . .

And later, by heart, Brahms'

Maria ging aus wandern
   So fern ins fremde Land
*Bis sie Gott den Herren fand.**

The walls of his shack are pasted with pages from the bible

voices underfoot and all around speak of a past
long ago that is now dark shapes and whispering
of howl-rent echoes far away and gone . . .

When the Dump-Keeper sings of hell and Solar Temples of Sea-galaxies
among all the slip-shod-shit and the golden picture frames

of city buildings breaking up, sliding with howls down
to the centre of the earth, he plays Grande Jeu, all the unisons —

all the black teeth of the harmonium, head back, his mouth wide

as a stone rainbow . . .

*Mary seeks through Jewry up and down
  until God, the Lord she found . . .

Stravinsky's / No Music

Behind the Abandoned Church,
faint bluesy-zingy lights from the Bingo Hall,

he dances like,
she dances like . . .

ripping out her eyelashes, she unravels her neck,
unscrews her breasts and throws them in the air —

while he pokes out his eyes,

with a stylish flick-knife,
slices off his scalp, throws them in the air:

eyes, breasts, planets, stylish flick-knife, scalp — circling among the lights:

she pulls out the glitterbugs in her nose,
tears out her tongue;

he jags out his earrings,
bites off his hands . . .

he dances like (for her)
she dances like

(flicking blood — for him)

eyes, lashes, neck, knife, scalp, hands, breasts, rings, tongue,
stars, planets, glitterbugs circling each other in the air

behind the Abandoned Church and the Bingo Hall tonight . . .

HOO-HAA! HOO-HA-HAA / Stravinsky's / no music / ceremony /

end of the first day of Spring.

Fast cars.
Snakes in the uterus.

(Soft trap of warm sperm also in savage burlesque of death)

12

Sea-mist

Buildings. Half seen / not.

Leviathan whale-bones / sea-mist
along the Esplanade:

Shh! of solar-prophesying sea-wrack,
sea-still and dead-white in a boater, hangs

its watery gut over a whelk-stall,
talking to a woman with a basket:

whiffs lay it on — smell of squalid beyond sea-wall
slime-breath on the cobbles

with grotesques and vaginal serpent-oozings through the sand . . .

vague figures, vague silences of weed — the slap! slap! under the rotted
    pier,

formless and swollen
where it washed ashore last night,

crawled

hairless, glittering with wet tiaras,
necklaces of teeth —

and a picture-poem to all the dead it ever swallowed . . .

The Air was Slab

The air was slab,
the Machair howled . . .

as the black sea rose
to meet its filthy mutant-sky —

brilliant / brilliant / brilliant
lightning strokes

lit the storm

o
v
e
r

a
n

inky lighthouse . . .

(white seagull pinned

                            its red heart on a skewer) . . .

                       * * *

— into floods . . .

— town waters —

drains
the dirty birthpill river sucking, blow-hard, sex-rich,

long whitecaps / greenwallow-lulls of snarling rotor-flames
in open rockfire spray and Smokeland-Kamikaze,

rubbish becomes flash —

a line of sunflash waves,
hollows race into razor-edge cliff-caves,

where minute blue spirits of the storm, cased in pure glass
chiming like mobiles —

        vanish into mirror infinity . . .

The Gull

Very brief government
    dispersal of winter birds,
            old / crippled hostelers,

               hunched moonface-children lurching,
    swirl over the promenade —

    taking sudden flight paths
      beyond clockworn streets
        and baleful Pentecost:

    sea-poisoned light / fog-cracks —

And it's all of a piece,
    schizophrenics will return,
circling cripples
          mount the sea, sea-heave, sea-birds:

desolation of wind-gust afternoon
    blow the drowned poor back on the beach;

(blood-streaks / wormholes
    dunlin piping
mudflats of the world)

they circle each other —
    a town-lost lurch of bubblegum ghosts —
        squashed faces through the clouds . . .

w / nowhere left to go: children.
papers, birds blow up like glass sparrows,

tap-tap of sticks.

An old man struggles over the town hall,
   caught in the trash-racks of the sky;

an urn spouts . . .

+ Time Lords morph through sunset windows
      over dirty floors and curled sandwiches
         in Le Café Postcard —

triumphal moment: a lone seagull —
  swoop of a last chip drawn through ketchup . . .

The Lilac Tree

... a bored upper class stifled by
inactivity and ennui.
Ox Comp to E.L.

Chekhov wrote —

> I long to be exiled to Siberia. One could sit by the Yenissey
> or Obi river and fish and on the ferry there would be nice
> little convicts, emigrants . . . Here I hate everything . . . this
> lilac tree in front of the river, these gravel paths . . .

With my plastic bags this morning,
I went into town via Ackland and the roadworks —

into Long Lane back of the Green Man, cut over
the Wasteland by Patel's Grocery and the Laundromat,
past the dead waving from the Job Centre, the Old Church —

walked by the cement works, the closed factory, the Undertakers —
so arriving at Main St. and Big W where I did my weekend shopping:
this being Monday, Saturday bread etc.

'. . . at fair everyday prices.'

Still looking for the Yenissey or the gravel path in the rain,
I returned North, West, South West, then East.

Dogs were silent in the downpour, a cat crouched under a car:
wisps of straw, Coke cans sailed past down the gutters.

To the corner of Sebastopol St., the distance was 4.7 kilometres.

Somewhere a kid was crying.

Enraged, someone opened a window
over a dead garden, bawling —

> '. . . shut your rotten-face up, bastard!'

— it was at *that* moment I thought: fried fish for dinner!

where rubbish blew past the gate

out of the Wasteland and its lost Obis —

and a small convict tree, rattling two black leaves,
leaned over the pavement

like a ghost . . .

tap-tapping on the window for the landlord . . .

Crows

Bobcat and tippers. Vain, beautiful and proud. Bogie drives.
They surge forward

behind sullen implosions of rain-soaked streets:

old people,

umbrella-huddled by plastic barriers,
watch their neighbourhood going in mud afternoon

of slow-motion physics, electrons flying off, atoms letting go.

                         Sebastopol St., Mafeking: dust pouring
through shattered windows,

nucleic acids dripping from architraves,

— flowing behind broken sinks, lavatories.

The machinery of state — tall buildings, mirror glass,
high-rise bureaucratic blueprints of the future,
anon. business / government faces staring from muddy puddles ...

a drear moment in which three crows polished blue / black
glide slowly past — eyes hooded, arrogant,

turn — suddenly veering up / vanish

into a pair of dirty trousers hanging from the sky ...

Ganbai! Drink and sing. How long is life ...

say the Chinese of the crude
and brutal politics of this violent planet ...

In Russia —

Hey! fuck your mother ...

The Outcrop

In Hokusai's print

'Eight parts bridge, Mikawa — a mist-shrouded hill outcrops
in the foreground: travellers stop to admire marsh iris . . .'

Here, under Bott St. and the housing estates
among lost mountains and laterites of Moon Hill,

ancient banded feldspawners and scrotum-screens,
upturned, rise through shattered ship-rock — inch

under North St., just feet under the Green Man, the Crash Repairs
and the Laundromat, before jaggedly outcropping

on the Wasteland by the Lethal Factory and the Cyclone Fence.

Year round, among heavy metal / thrash / grunge —
surrounded by abandoned fig trees,

nautsch-rags, rivers of broken church-glass and tatty flootchers —

Hokusai might have drawn the background to the Rock with a fine brush —

'Pines and Waves over the Chemical Works '
'Urinals at Night by the Old People's Home and the Closed Hospital'
'Past the Sewage Works with Winds and Hurricane Twigs across the Plain'

In rain, unpleasant belly-snatch, black-wet-smeary-red — a landmark

noted in senior school project books for its *Geographical Significance*
— as instanced, tonight, by vile winds from the Carboniferous —

and, high above Marilyn Close, melting guitars, hot mists

billowing across the moon with cyanide colours

(not just your ordinary

japanese tat-grotty-gob-suck-
sentimentally-knackered-potch-

sky-poop)

The Colts

Suddenly, it's midnight!

A lone retiree in a Promised Land,

a small gray man stands under the stars,
marking the last moments

of his working life as a factory hand.

    The clock strikes! Not a muscle moves —

but faster'n you could bet,
faster than the Kid —

those two mother-shover Colts he's been saving —

Yugoslav-Mex-Wop! And *Pow!* Into the sky

Merdre! Jesu Christi, por Dios!
Both hands, lead! yellow! the moon!

Doc Holiday of the suburbs,
Big-Buffalo-John Wayne-Bill shouting Hi! Yip! EEEEE! YIIII!

in multicultural Chineseyankeeblackfootsioux

as he gallops around the block, waving his Stetson at the world.

Sagitarius! Pow! Stars! Pow! Black holes, Halley, Hercules and Herschel!
  Pow!

  (legs spread wide there among the wagons, blowing smoke from his guns)

But he gives no sign.
He just stands there looking at the stars.

Later, he goes to bed and sleeps.

Orchard St. sleeps.
The world sleeps.
The moon sleeps.

Meanwhile, back in the Last Chance Saloon . . .

Harvest

Summer wanes, humming Schiller's Ode to Joy —

quietly wafting stone grasshoppers and gnats;
    the soft mmm / mmm / of choirs rolling this Autumnal

moon

over

wheatfields . . .

where giant moths with striped eyelids
of the Zodiac

keep trying to steal the revolutionary night.

— And the fourteen thousand
billion billion unemployed millennia of stars
needed to complete the names of God,
wheel light years over glittering oceans, sshhh! sshhh! sludge-ebb

of lost lorry parts, wastelands and forever soul-journeys.

Small Lowery-stick-figures stare up
from poisoned shadows — industrial wreckage
of planetary factories curved like the gigantic ribs
of an upturned boat. Among lost worlds,

a child's muffled cry, dead-weight and visions
give form to night, to distant traffic, cat-yowls
in Ur-syllables from the Kaddish . . .

Groping through rubble, the dead stumble: a drunk heaves
vowel-howls on the road, a red wine gush-fall
as he lurches off a rainbow dangling
from the corner of his mouth . . . a song without words,

in which a shooting star suddenly streaks itself out like a fag-end:
and all the poetry of the night rushes in —
a dog leaps in a backyard, shouting Moon! Moon!
a golden mist rolls upriver over rusting docklands —

And somewhere — a tiny goods train with silver buffers
carrying the bones of children with unblinking eyes,
goes round and round . . . whistling, whistling.

In the fall of rust-crash-shunting over factory rooftops —
and the soft, faraway hum / mmm / of choirs —

you can almost smell the wheat ripening . . .

Butterflies swing . . .

Evil Big Mouth on hostile terrain, Giant Legs
and officials shouting

putting their smack-down on the streets again:

past the Wasteland's blowing rubbish,
graffiti artists, last night, at work on Main St. . . .

with green-purple spraycan wombmen and strange isotopes

in 'Escape from
                    Nameless Malevolence
                    into the Future . . .'

and
            'Psychedelic Holes
                        Of Fear
                        In Sojourning Horsemen of the Apocalypse . . .'

— Sometime (through all-day drift of the town, copper-sulphate clouds
and Blue Institutes in Brown Dreaming) were zapped!

sandblasted off like freaked out heirlooms of the wind —
Pollock's Abstract Agonies, Schizoid-Fractals and Disassociated
    Modernism

among Trumpeting from the Swamps . . .

Now ooze-red shadows of closed factories purple into sky-pool-paint,
butterflies swing over the Wasteland . . .

sweet broken glass gives back its light

— a fingerpost for Rembrandt!

where an old man, sweat on his face,
is pissing on the wall back of the Hoo Fong chippie . . .

Flash-pulse

Velociraptor —

street
thunder-
poem

ultimate sex,

0–150 mph
in 4.9
seconds . . .

Jurassic spinoff —

smashed Indy cars and stars
espaliered across horizons

in unexpurgated
skull-solar-energy-fields

of flash-pulse and a faceful of killer-teeth:

home of the west wind
and the headless fossil-men . . .

Boulevard

Sun's jagged triphammer *whang! bangs* /
shattering / city's impenetrable light . . .

blind rays zoom off in flash /

of business dominant skyscrapers erupting numbers —
fabulous fountains of high octane preference shares,

in satellite-doom-time, pavement-shimmer-
café-time / theatre of satyrs

through which youth wanders —
the wet placenta of each nostril quivering,

testing the ambience

as one and all they join the happy throng
along the Boulevard of Dreams.

They're rehearsing lines where the strange
powers of Pepsi and Destiny apply . . .

  'Vomit — you've got to lick their vomit!
  'Shit — you've got to smell their arseholes . . .'

  Behind the store —

collective cool stare,
Kaddish for all applicants —

'. . . we'll give you a call . . .'

YA!
YEAH!

Sneakers.
Leather jackets.

Total street cred as yet uneaten by the tribal weird . . .

Count on it —

more black poetry of the weightless spirit
considering its next quantum leap among the stars . . .

Erotic

Klimt of the Golden Brush painting sex / honey / money —

    sex-money-hungry-gold snakes coiled in honey-gold sheets:

— payment in any currency —
Stock Exchanges, Moneymarts . . .

Klimt painting the biggest cock on Wall St.,

Klimt with his telescope fixed on the hairiest cunt circling the moon —

and sex-honey, sex honey dripping
Niagaras of viagras, asps in gasps
moans in Romes . . .

erections and insurrections, bourse after bourse,
London, Paris, Tokyo, New York — night storm-trumpets,

whiplash-stars, necks of tourists —
and lightning! flickering backwards and forwards

in the D. Jones / Nasdaq / True Garden of Eden World Sex Gigantic
Championships for the Randiest, Raunchiest, most Board-Sitting,
Company Owning, Asset-Stripping-Carpet Bagging
Ball-Bag-Semen Pistol on Earth . . .

until the last stroke of the racket:

until TV of the Universe falls on its knees screaming Vas! Vas! Vas!

. . . through the window at night as you listen to what the thunder says,
           " after the torchlight red on sweaty faces . . ."

after the last gold / gasp / groan / sex / seethe in the storm,
after the last Shantih   Shantih   Shantih rolls into distance . . .

turn on the radio for more news of the All Ords. and Ten Year Bonds . . .

and watch for gold at sunrise again, that first erotic gleam
of more wet-gobstopping, whoremongering, share-grabbing,
internet-sonovabitching, cash down-plastic-card-homage to the System
which is the deadliest, most beautiful thing in the world.

And pure Klimt.

Waaaap!

Riding a Testosterone Special, first light . . .

Class 91 Electric, 84 ton, 6090 hp

Waaaap!

Failed brokers at work on laptops at 140 mph —
death's head Levites and extinct souls:

The train rocks:

hedge funds, variable long and short exposures,
illiquidities, Pictet funds, risk appetites . . .

Flash! a bridge, a pond.

First light and a sun spear-shatter / dazzle.

The Japanese market,
Malabar Management
1 Boulevard Royal L 2449 Lux.

Skywalkers in crimson surround us; between night and morning,
a long bridge, where star-swarms vanish into time

and the train rounds its last long run through cows / pollen / elves.
That deathbed watch between planets,

a perfect moment for high-end handsets / Symbian Op. Systems
to leave purple / gold

                                        / blood

Oestrogen claw marks in the sky.

It's all of a piece

— torn welcome posters,

glimpses of Straddlin, Izzy and the Ju Ju Hounds,
the Greyhound bus slides past

city outskirts, breeze blocks, portakabins —
black flowers of the tenements:

It's all of a piece: coming home! travelling since dawn.

People getting ready: fingering their bags.

Viets., Lebs., Blacks, old women
grey / white / black / yellow faces coming home.

All coming home — watching the streets,
the Methodist Church, the Bingo Hall,

by the railway, the freightyards, the Poison Factory,
by Mrs T's. back fence with ribbons in its hair.

It's morning.   It's the first Greyhound bus:

*from under rotten windows, closed shopfronts,
the side of derelict warehouses —*

*where first sun-shafts flashing windows lift the backstreets
like a trumpet to their lips*
                              and blow!

Closing their eyes   as they lift their faces to their parent star

                    & blow!

Until everything becomes a metaphor.

Corbusier's Patch

They of the twisted car-yard gothic,

cankered, squat-eaten trees
deep in skull-neighbourhood:

cut one, they all bleed — blackmail,

knuckle-dusters, tyre-irons, buckshot —
a century's business history bared, mayors, councilors,

committees, cop-extortions, drug money-deals . . .

One step here through the void
and you can hear them all screaming in the dark;

and it's every night — howl of Tech house and Electrolash,
lights swerving off tree-trunks, shadowy people

who fade back into deeper shadows, echoing stairs
and bubble-wrapped filth . . . a roar of bones,

traffic, clattering streets.

It shoots on through and then returns, Corbusier's High-Rise
Concrete, the sodium-lit grin, the deal,

the double-cross, the dead-cat bounce.

Old trees on the periphery flash-lit / flash-lit
are like the ghosts of the beginning and forever —

chopped into, mutilated by scrap-yards, whorehouses,
with here and there the blossom of killing ivy.

They stand there
smelling their own armpits —

Mmmm! Mmmm!

while a breeze rides a flock-dirty moon among the leaves,
blowing a few this way-that among

the kerb-crawling traffic of yet another brutal century passing through . . .

Dead Men's Clothes

Witnesses and Mormons: missionaries
bent against the wind, crawling

over the great bell curve of the Estate . . .

In town, crying of winter storms
as coffins passed

derelict factories
tall houses

half-dark
and waves almost swamping
the Charity Shop

with dead men's clothes for sails.

They said — '. . . we'd never have known what to do
that year without the dead men's clothes —

and the great steady singing in the night . . .'

As the sky oscillated,
trees shouted a warning . . .

flash / white
flash / white

electric fields over the roar of waters
between clouds we'd never seen before . . .

Maw

Beast-ial
turd —

rotting digestion of slaughterhouse

murder-murder —

obesity:

Mouth shouts, Maw gobble-gobbles juices / belly rumbles,
world yellow-fat factories roll down the gutter:

Schlup! Schlup! The Giant American Gas-house Dream —
Chomp-grind of black teeth, Maw pounding

on edible / inedible / raw bible-bashing clouds for more
immense blubby-squish-peristaltic-prairie-factories,

with shovel-gob-hup-shovel-hup-hamburger-gurgle,
bones, metal, rocks — leviathan-planet-boom!

MoonMarsStars!

all hot belly-bump, fart and gut-drop's midnight whistle,
crash-lurch of impossible world-voyages hurtling through the sky . . .

praising God . . .

Clouds

Aeons ago — Coleridge, Wordsworth ... *clear rains falling /*

'Clouds Worshipping the Invisible ...'
              'Nature and Truth ...'

Constable's vast-woolly
cumuli, gray slurry at the edges —

'... escape to evanescence in the chiaroscuro ...'

              on they went over hill and dale — Cirrus, Cloud Streets,
              Lee Waves, Breaking Billows —

              all Claude territory: Aeneas at Delos, the classical unified
              geometry

(lines hidden now by inversions over the city where the Freeway
vanishes from the Mesozoic High Plains to horizons over

Precambrian fault blocks and outwash deposits in the suburbs)

Turner painted the smoggy way an old bag-woman

is going now as she ducks under a pair of rotten lungs
hanging from a line,

past Cheap-as-chips and Rent-a-telly,

wheeling her pram through boulders and gravels of the Eocene
towards sci-fi horizons raging with Nitrogen dioxide and PCB's.

In an urban heat-island of benzene-aldehyde fog,
site of a vandalized urinal,

she picks up this free, trashed Microsoft Manual,

with giraffe stickers,

hung from rusting traffic lights / kicked in door . . .

(left to wipe your ass on, Gran'ma!)

It's the Empire Game-Plan; the too-soon Water War's Invasion
of Silicon-Valley-Planetary-Dust Bowl Mutants Inc . . .

shadows with weird mouths descending
on long ladders from the clouds —

black night as the old woman knock! knocks on
a cardboard dugout in the suburbs:

Is that you, Gran'ma?
Is it really you?

Snap / click

A streetlight-trashcan —

bucket of circle-shadows,

tremors
on almost still life —

lost mumbling-limbs
in mini-

lashes of chemical death.

In Pentax night, the carpark is deserted.

Then —
the cockroach's legs start to pedal again.

Beside a throwaway razor, a strip of Styrofoam —

a black chocolate cream-wrapper
stares through a half-eaten dark

in a wet Japanese liquorice box . . .

                        * * *

Stop! Click!

on this Zyklon B moment — a storm coming in,

mad violence of decomposed Circe body-fluids
in typhoid chill,

widow-killer in black smoke-clouds

that shrieks to a gobstopped O
west of the City:

flame-glint of a gutter-butterfly
on a yogurt carton's carved quick-set-shimmer-fire.

It's the quickness of the eye — quick curving light
from the Universe — tail-end of a meteorite over the City,

an Ektachrome 160, 1/4, f 5.6

catches a failed moon rotten with fungus,
black sections, planks falling

in drift and see-saw over the Rubbish Dump . . .

* * *

From the cries of lost souls in the dark — this glimpsed
in the common prayer-book of all people:

— a starburst lens —
top of a tower-block / night / on the hill /

broken windows / hee-haw of a cop car /

in flash / fall, turning

over a million houses —

a
single
snow-
flake
drifts

through the immensity of space . . .

Movie

Instant morning flash
with rain!

        on opening the curtains — a cemetery skims by;

        streakt

white

ZOOMS!

Everywhere you go —
reminders —

the beginning is in the end:

        condensed animal matter

(one cemetery can outsmart,
 a thousand streets . . .)

        — epitaphs, deaths, godly fetishes
        — with corpse-schmooze,

belly-boo with yech glop and gangrenous plumbing . . .

If Tarot cards and the city jump one way,
the hearse is there before,

if fateful Cabala turn on themselves —
a giant trumpet blows from the clouds:

— skyful of nettles, urns, crosses,
broken bottles —

all sheet / shimmer / fire over a church spire.

After rain . . . mirrors! flash-fotos! cameras!

a million cancer puddles
laced with dogshit, rubbish, heart attacks

splashed by traffic — glistening upside-down to sunset,
angels, Jacob's Ladder, people —

all gawking at

the same movie.

Three Views of a Mountain

    — sunset, end of Canal Street —
      up the cloud-mountain's easy
with Kano . . .

a pair of six-fold screens,

gold leaf, with pheasants —

a stone boat
travels through evening-waterfalls . . .

high over Woolworth's and the Bottle shop —
through an icy pass, snowgeese in a whirling cloud —

the Bodhisattva Kannon
on a lotus throne
of green flames

crowned by dangerous peaks . . .

all night —

looking neither left
nor right,

grey rocks
from the summit,

pilgrims

in frozen mist,

roll silently down Main St.,

on their long journey towards an unknown sea —

Around the Nine-Storey Swastika Mountain

Mt. Kailas the holy — whose Eastern face
is crystal, the South sapphire, the West
ruby, and the North gold . . .
Legend

With stains of sapphire and ruby among smashed,
still-vibrating cymbals,

conch shells, giant gold trumpets in the snow —

Tibetan prayer-flags strain in frozen wind,
dreaming inscapes of death-blue-ice.

The higher — '. . . *there arose in me light* — '

The Buddha's last birth

in spellbound void for hours: marzipan colours
and hydrogen-raptors whistle through the diaspora,
fall like black specks from the sky,

distant voices echo / return bringing snow-cries
of the dead like so many soul-curved instruments of rock.

For mass-upon-mass, snows
glitter down towards India

where Death Puppets dancing with Guru Trakpo,
the Black-Hatted Sorcerer, stream up
through folds in the earth's crust — by falling over peaks

into rebirth as through some nebula at the edge of time — return —
dancing flash! metal! dolls! —

blinding rays of a blue star . . .

Mountain Big-Rock

Counting last moments . . . sunrise zero minus ten —

Tourist buses / marzipan spirits, true names of trees —

Minus five — Wanambi snake slithers away:

Solar

      d
      a
      w
      N

    . . . Blush . . .

DOUBLE-FLASH

. . . with hijacked visions of eternity /
crimsonfireburntcarmine /
dripping out of a yen, drachmae / yankee-euro dollar-dawn /

— a Wurlitzer-whooosh AAAHH! as Mountain Big-Rock starts turning,
— sweeping, surfing the sun-tips, whipping and singing like a top
  in the Fantastiche Ever-Ever Uluru-Moneyball Sky:

faster and faster / rolling in it, being baptized in it —

Cash Waterfall,
Ship of Gold,
Sky-full of Diamond Didgeridoos . . .

as round it goes, millions upon millions — entrepreneurs,

shrieks / multicultural toilets / buses, Outback hotel pools,
  mini-bar drunks, escapees to the Red Centre in www dot com.
Valley of the Winds, Messengers of the Kerungra, Sacred Loritdja Foods . . .

Terrified sand-turtles shriek at the sky: desert hawks plunge
   as sky-vents flame into a future that is already past:

faster and faster!

singing the planet . . .
leaving the planet . . .

singing the planet . . .
leaving the planet . . .

Cowdust

At 30,000 ft,
a farewell sunset:

on
every
cloud

a Shining Buddha . . .

Dazzling Heaven of the Four Great Kings
poured through peacock feathers:

mist of rainbow colours and joss-sticks

lit by radiance
and the Formless Worlds / whirl / changing

into vortex / brass temple bells. Hidden below,

the poor man's hour of Cowdust
floats mote-like. Clay huts,

cows and bicycles / smells of cooking / dal, a few chillis,
some jaggery . . .

'Give a son to my wife,
 And a daughter to my buffalo . . .' is the saying

Or '. . . if the well dries,
    . . . if the Monsoon is late
    . . . if the crops fail!

In cities — lepers fade into shadows,
            pavement sleepers huddle for warmth:
            alleyway beggars squat for a last shit . . .

Ramakrishna spoke of ecstasy as the consciousness of an unknown
Universe that is awakened while the awareness of the ordinary
Universe is asleep . . .

One conclusion, he declared, — *that of*
Living in the constant Presence of God . . .

One by one, the Buddhas vanish — an invisible 747 dot-drifts a vapour trail
through sky-frozen-pink fading to bitter purple — whispering:

D.I.N.N.E.R. I.S. S.E.R.V.E.D.

D.I.N.N.E.R. I.S. S.E.R.V.E.D . . .

Waiting

From the North comes Peace
from the South-West, Mother, Practicality and Family Oneness

bathing blue trees in Dawn-park

by the hospital — where an old Vietnamese woman
waits on an iron bench beside a lake in the gardens
for news of her grand-daughter.

In terms of Feng Shui —

the fortunate stars having shone like swastikas all night,
now fade into first pink cloudways in a trial of strength . . .

She watches a heron fly past.
A first sun-blade, flashing from a tall building in the sky,

suddenly deflected, becomes a creature of wild crimson, a lake
of green, red, purple zing-zang-ripples —
all ricocheting into star-burst

mirrors, helium fluids by the Herbarium / mystic antagonists /
caves of white echoes spang from the glasshouses . . .

Backwards and forwards,
whang! rainbow-shards!
soul orbits crashing through the ether;

they surround the old woman
lifting her to her feet,
spirits with red eyelids,

her ancestors, come floating over the lake,
jade shadows with radium pouring from their eyes —

'CON GÁI /
LÃ CON TRAI . . .'

a girl / it's a boy . . .

The Train

The Howard Government's '... cruel, inhuman,
and degrading treatment of refugee children in its care ...'
The Human Rights Commission 2004*

No luggage-toy-train —
crayon-train's on the line,

Purple-yellow-crayon train hoo — hoos! down

(from the
Migrant Detention Centre)

Children at rattling carriage windows,
GIANT FACES LOOKING OUT! ...

green-wheel / yellow-wheel-train ...
covered with flowers:

(high razor-wire fences in the dark)

Refugee train
tickety-tacking-up-along
down ...

crayonmen on stilts,
strange whistling creatures from moon caves ...

black wings, blue lips ...

swoop through
poison-fall of the sun — screaming —

G'baaack! G'baaack!

THROUGH THE TUNNEL

THE ENGINE PUFFS

3 lemons
4 gold oranges ...

*Between July 1999 and June 2003, 2184 refugee children in Australia spent an average
of 20 months 11 days behind razor-wire and electrified fences ...

Over the Lake

In Spring-yellow-time,

among falling blossom by the lake,
Mrs Li meditates in the lotus position:

a Qi-storm —

vortex of heavenly energy,
drawn from the centre of the Universe,

swirl-dances golden clouds,
sweeping and swaying

over the city, among the trees —

cosmic particles her skin,
instantly absorbs.

While her third eye clicks like a shutter, sacred power,
drawn to the Wheel of the Fulan in her stomach,

spin-glitters: mystic / yellow / gold / blue / black / red

transmuting *Qi* into virtuous *Gong*
 (in raw mysteries of blood and light, tranquil but conscious mind

Strengthening Pillar-Shaped Divine Powers)

Her beautiful third eye,
Tianmu —

a mirror, flashes and turns, seeing all things to the end of the world;

Qi swirls, her *Fulan spins a thousand colour-shades* . . .

as heavenly dimensions
encompass and the Universe throbs *in / out / in / out,*

now smaller, now larger,

a spun jewel caught in the a moment of mystical union
with epochs of the calyx and the shape of smoke . . .

Dazzled by the lake, the sun's hands point straight down
to become *Shuang Long Xia Hai* —

Two Dragons Diving into the Sea.

Samcheong-sunsets

Dreaming Samcheong-sunsets — Sarong islands and veiled seas
  drag me suddenly over a Cézanne-edge —

baked bean lids / children falling through windows of air into
  blue-prams and green-steepled

gables — all commerced into pure razzle-dazzle
  supermarket colour-puddle —

and a vomited-up strawberry-layered-purple-beige-chocolate
  icecream Extry Speshull Space Lifter

dropped by showery air-spirits to compose this scene . . .

Ah! Celestial! Sunfall! Flash! It arches over — bubblegum ghosts,

pure rainbow-shining, Satyrs and strange priests
  with hairy haunches, in psychedelic getaway

from paintbox carpark:

three naked shopping trolleys / hitching a lift / to anywhere . . .

Labyrinth

Snuffed stars . . .
    a world, a word —

    vowels, a noxious dream-dirge:

    a cargo of dead voices
    clutches its children like voodoo dolls

    in a wallowing derelict. Lost
    in deadly reflections of a labyrinth,

    yellow streaks fall like burning paper on the ocean.

    Calmed between past and future —

    rimfire and unkillable sun-boosters, fierce X-rays,
    hiss . . . light dazzles back fracturing

    the sky: the compass swivels, hammer-knocks
    on a dead engine, the freighter drifts,

    scaly-iron hums softly to itself . . .

    tides, peacock distances and miasmic refugee shit
    inch, backwards / forwards like a fly crawling upside down

    over the immense blue globe of the world . . .

Daydreaming

Lost in thought, Mr A Sidharta, Jay St. Australia,
walking home after work,

daydreams eating *ayam goreng*

from a street stall in Blok M — or Sulawesi-style *ikan baka*,
pavement-dining, Jakarta —

just as old Mrs Nguyen
shuffles past —

daydreaming *her* trance among brilliant birds and butterflies
in U Minh forest by the rice fields . . .

watching a grey crane

which is

        about

              just

                    about —

to

. . . Splasshh! lands on one ski!

unfurls a coloured sun-umbrella . . .
and quietly

        peck!

          peck!

            pecks!

When the ripples with mangrove leaves lap Mr Sidharta's feet
on Jalan Kendal —

and an orange three-wheel *bajaj* passes Mrs Nguyen
and the grey crane in the Mekong Delta —

hoot-tooting at the sky,

they all think the monsoon has arrived . . .

Sharks

Melancholy passage
when sailing's done —

as white gulls peel from the wound . . .

Shark Emperors in wave-time of the godhead
shatter the vast sun-penumbra

with infarct army of invincible shadows:

the sea boils, shuddering cries

and purple crystals fall into the sunset
where gaudy souls, cased in glass and charcoal,

swim like coloured butterflies towards an invisible shore

and a giant manta ray, torn by gold,
flaps into the sky.

Iridescent froth and blue bubbles in free-fall and gay-cloud —

history of decomposed violence and clobber
among flotsam and H_2O bobbing towards sunset

in last voyage of a solitary lifebelt talking to the sky . . .

Dead Soldier Blues

Bind up their heads, mister TV man —

they say war is a proving ground

Ummmm hmmmm

Mmmmmm

they say — that glory, we'll never see its like again:

Old men mmmm mmmm

old men, nothing left to do, laying the black mouth on you,
going round and round
marching round and round,

laying the black mouth on you with smashed guns pointing at the sky,
empty guns left behind keep pointing at the sky.

Mmmmmmm mmmmmmm

Hmmmmm.

Old men, wired for war-time sounds,
old men marching round,

rust and bullets pouring from their mouths . . .

My kids don't want to see
No! I don't want to see

Bind up their heads. Mister TV man,
Bind up their heads

Ummmmm hmmmmm yes . . .

I've got the dead soldier blues and I don't want to see those old-man
    dreams . . .

The dead-soldier blues I've got listening to wingbeats beating in my soul.

The dead soldier blues is all . . .

Orgasmatron

Driving the Steel Rains of Heaven —

God-Winds in third world, mud-brick-village killing grounds . . .

a B2 Stealth break-dance,
maelstrom-vortex

in electrifying mayhem of

Diehard Original.

The hiss of light is everywhere! warped riffage,

+ hostile arrogance! insane howl-poetry
of sky-blowing dust through empty bones,

world to —

tally in awe,

Berzerk!
Live!
Head on!

Red flames in a wilderness
of mirrors —

Kab — ooon! Kerraang!

Kid-orgasmatrons, body-yell-parts

in rage-for-world-order, mindmyth
and piledriving spinal tap . . .

War's long-haul, no end to dreams'
inexhaustible blood-black pouring

through windows / watched spatter on glass,

bonechill

evil eye

ouchless TV

Answer / don't

Answer the phone / don't . . .

Old folks in mind-fear of brr-brr
home invasions — money-gabble —

and 3 am calls,

shuffle, half-naked,

peering through glass at illegitimate horror:

bizzy-bizness, crazy interludes at the window,
poundings on the door:

giants sleeping in weed-lots,
cardboard boxes . . .

Weird sentinels of the night

sweep through twilight valleys
with huge lenses and spectra

in dislocation of dream-states — just listening

to phone / brr / brr-rr / like moths going round

and round the moon.

When old people
have answered enough

phone-junk-yell-echoes,

they wrap themselves in cockleshell leaves
and float out

through green willow-tunnels
high above the white waterfalls of time . . .

among sheet-winged purples / yellows / small blues /
Admirals / dipping, soaring,

clouds of them fluttering . . .

Hole

I was charmed . . .

(pulling aside curtains of unknowing
spider-strewn dark)

Old Mother Hubbard,

and a child's violin in
a second-hand shop —

Riddle-me-ree / See-saw Marjorie Daw /
Little bird sang trilloo, trilloo —

But its feet dangled like Alice
when I picked it up — through the hole

bashed in its back
where the music used to be:

inside / a Victorian bustle, taffeta rustle,

pussy in the well /

stomach with black teeth
licking a flypaper in the dark / killed by the bus . . .

crowded me through gloom like broken pianos:

strange garlicky creatures with faery wings,

elephant-foot umbrella stands, all humming the same tune . . .

Changing House

Soot-soot!

the little slant-eyed Fireplace Dragon in the dark

. . . and behind the door

                    ZZZt!

                                        PPhhh!

                    WAAAAH!

          In the corner flashing . . .

                              a tall greasy hat
                              w / blackheads.

Prophetic utterances

of
an
electric
cooker . . .

Aroma-doma

— love you, Mr Enteritis Man,

all that aroma-doma, blubby-flop-flab, Note blubby etc. Leave.
odour-loader-bubble blab . . .

sizzle-splash
sausage-char-chips

with long strips of cholesterol dangling from the sky:

Old Guggle-Guts'

Franchisee baseball cap's back-to-front,

flat splat of a spatula as black gas billows
hackle-crackle of fat — packed

blue-green energy

unwinding from a giblet-bucket
buzz-buzzz

back of the counter:

they pass you down the street —
late again —

eating from greasy papers
high-heels click-clack

wobble-fart, wobble-fart, wobble-fart.

It skids underfoot,
slides down the wall:

When you open your mouth to gob-rid a gristle piece —

two flies in failed
suction-boots

fall in . . .

The Drain

There's always Grumpelschon Gigantibus
trailing a broken fence —

but thinking small — think
Oleaginus Vulgaris and bin-slime —

or cold schmooze
on cat turd:

under a frouche-cup by the railings,
lee of a beer can and rotten chippy papers,

swarming over rubbish, bricks, glass, in the rain
filling space and what to do with it —

Jollycurious Minimus Accelerando,
and Burglarious Purpurea with Fake Jake

and little Weasel Blackmouthed Bastardino
rampant everywhere:

it's their world: demolition sites, vacant lots . . .

and it's how another day falls just now —
or the end of it — estuaries

of street lights glinting on gutter-pools,
fag-ends with rubbish,

behind the footy ground, whole neighbourhood's

sip-sip,
cold drip . . .

into Goo-bloo,

bottom of a street-drain
by the Thrift Store,

— Boggy Town lavatory water.

Little Bo-Peep / worm dance all puckered up.

In the Field of Green Beanz Cows

Garn thuck-mud!
Garn!
      muck-thup! Huckmup

gubber . . . bubbery, bobber . . .

Hey, ducky! Here duckyduckyducky . . .

Tum thunk
Tum thunk

Hup chudder and gob.

Hup now! Hup!

Good nod, good chod.

Wok!wok!   Wokwok! Dog, good nod.

Trokka-tractor-kahatcha-hatcher-hatchaka . . .

Round and round

Then — Upsy!! Hey! / Hap / blub sludge!

Happerschnitz und Frierschlitz
in green beanz field of blubberschnutz . . .

Hey Podge! Hey Nodge!

Slobber-gobber
and gate screech.

Good wopsy, good nopsy,

Schiessen und shitten plop blobs, plop-dops.
Milky thick-whizz blubber

gobsnatch slime
          mooo!

Mumble miaoww

        hibblesnitch!   Butty-splash!

All Dawn

— and what a morning's misty-moisty

smiles in this all-dawn fieldforest-edge,
looking, listening to

tinkle,
triangle-
chimes:

so comfortable, these moo-swaying, patchwork,
apple-cushion-sweetcuddle of

potato-sacks
eyetips,
lashes.

Of course, good-humoured hobblegob sludge. Horn-tossing,
vast astonishment, belly-grumble wonder at finding themselves
in this new / this every moment —

sweet-chiming planet, this archetypal / everything /
you, the mist rising — in one pleasing image —

udderfly,

nettleswitch,

pastoral . . .

Elegy in a Country Churchyard

Says Gubby Slack
to Filthy Ears . . .

says Fuggin Green to Wobby Gug:

(there, in the corner of the cemetery,
they grow thinner than mushrooms —

and high they are, very ghostly white and high,
among the branches in the mist,

over the gravestones in the dark)

IFFANUMPTHN says Gubby Slack
IFFANUMPTHN to Wobby Gug.

WWGLZZZYPS says Fuggin Green
WWGLZZZYPS to Filthy Ears

Some say it's frogs —
But I've seen
The Talking Heads
Swivelling and nodding in the dark

While they yobbed me leery with their eyes.

They're ectoplasm — Puff-heads with poison
Whose diamond souls have reached singularity.

IFFANUMPTHN! IFFANUMPTHN! IFFANUMPTHN!
WWGLZZZYPS! WWGLZZZYPS! WWGLZZZYPS!

By the lychgate bottom of the hill

where mist is thicker than gangrene —

still sadly missed
by Dirty Hair, Thin Legs etc., . . .

you can hear Old Hupplebonce, Puttywhackle and Huffenschmak

pissing on their graves . . .

By the same author

<u>Collage</u>

Peter Lloyd

ISBN 1 86254 570 7

'Real craft, raw power – demands repeated reading.'
Anthony Lawrence, Poetry Book Club of Australia

'Strength and macabre wit.'
Rudi Krausmann, *Imago*, University of Queensland

'Of the highest quality and completely original.'
John Millett, *Poetry Australia*

'Charged with unique and magnetic style.'
David Kelly

<u>Black Swans</u>

Peter Lloyd

ISBN 1 86254 398 4

'The surreal visual imagery is outstanding, often converting
the other senses into the visual.'
Graham Rowlands

For more information visit www.wakefieldpress.com.au

Wakefield Press is an independent publishing and
distribution company based in Adelaide, South Australia.
We love good stories and publish beautiful books.
To see our full range of titles, please visit our website at
www.wakefieldpress.com.au.

Wakefield Press thanks Fox Creek Wines
and Arts South Australia for their support.